MW01124129

MODERN ACTIVIST

A

BOOK

BY

ANDY TILLY

MODERN ACTIVIST

Published by Xi Publishing House
Printed in the United States of America

TABLE OF CONTENTS

FOREWARD

I couldn't help but smile when I saw the title of this book. Modern Activist. It captures in two words the passion of my heart, and I believe the heart of Jesus. His famous prayer that says, "may your Kingdom come, may your will be done, on Earth as it is in heaven," has been my prayer for my little corner of the world. In God's Kingdom, the hungry get fed, the sick find healing, injustice is made right, enemies forgive one another, people walk in freedom and people far from God surrender their hearts to Jesus Christ.

It's one thing to ask God to bless the hurting. It's quite another thing to ask God to make me a blessing to the hurting. Sometimes I forget that God uses me to bring His Kingdom to earth. He's given me the Holy Spirit and according to His word the same power that conquered the grave lives in me. I am equipped and empowered to do what He did and to affect change in the world around me.

Without question Jesus was an activist. He was a force for change in the name of God. The world has never been the same since Jesus showed up. Can the same be said about us?

I've known Andy for many years and watched him lead our students here at Cross Timbers. His heart for young people is obvious. He dreams big dreams and trusts God to use him for His glory. Students are catching the vision of being world changers and neighborhood changers. The Holy Spirit is shaping, leading and equipping these young men and women in inspiring ways. Their world is changing. They are changing. Read carefully the words that Andy has written. Study the passages he mentioned. Ask Jesus to use you and the Holy Spirit to lead you.

You'll never regret a life lived for God's glory!

Toby Slough
Lead Pastor
Cross Timbers Community Church

INTRODUCTION

At nineteen years old, I stood at the tailgate of a truck packed with everything I owned. The truck was loaded with a few boxes of clothes and some memories of the last ten years or so. I was about to pull away from my parents' 100-acre farm in Oklahoma, and everything that I had known to embark on a journey of a lifetime. I had barely graduated from high school with a perfect 2.1 GPA—not too impressive by many people's standards, especially coming from a home with a schoolteacher as a mom. Now, I had heard from God to take this journey, yet to be honest, I was unsure of what the future might hold for an average, not-too-smart and somewhat rebellious kid.

Standing there looking over the pipe and cable fence I had painted several times over the years, I stared at my parents horses. I couldn't help but think, "Am I making a huge mistake?" This was home, a safe place in which everything seemed to make sense. It was where my friends lived and would remain to build their own lives. I knew deep within me, however, that something was stirring, something I couldn't explain. It was a feeling, an emotion and a calling that God had something bigger for me than working at a ranch, cleaning horse poop and feeding cattle all day. Don't get me wrong, there's nothing wrong with that. But deep down, I felt a calling for something different, a calling to go where I hadn't been before, even if I didn't exactly know where the journey would take me.

My mind was racing. *Should I stay or should I go? What if I was wrong? What if I was making a terrible mistake that would take years to fix? What if I thought I had heard from God and it wasn't really God at all?* That's when my dad came alongside me, put his hand on my shoulder and looked this scared teenager in the face. My dad and I have always been close, and I respected what he had to say, even if I had often gone the opposite direction in the past. Standing side-by-side, he told me something I will never forget. He said, "Andy, you can do anything that God has called you to! Nothing is impossible for you."

I wasn't thinking about the fact that he was speaking Scripture over me, but in that moment I had a choice: Did I believe what he said, or didn't I? Did I believe that I could do anything God had called me to, or did I play it safe and unpack the truck? While I bet my mother wishes I had unpacked the truck, I had to move on.

I closed the door to the vehicle and watched my dad in the rearview mirror as I pulled away. I remember thinking that I might just be the dumbest kid around, but I made a choice. I believed my dad—or you could say I believed Scripture like never before! From that day forward, even in the hardest times, I knew nothing was impossible for me if God was in it. The words my father spoke that day changed everything, and I am eternally grateful.

My dad doesn't remember much of that conversation, and that's ok. We don't always remember the most powerful moments we have in people's lives, probably because they are God-moments. They don't seem like much to us, but to the person on the receiving end, they change everything. During my particular moment, God spoke through my dad and shattered any limitations I had previously put on myself.

Traveling down the old dirt road I had driven back and forth for years, I thought to myself, "This is it." It was time to make things happen and be all that God had called me to be. But the bigger question was: *What?* What exactly had God called me to be? What did He want do with my life? What had He gifted and prepared me for? I couldn't answer those questions then, but I can now. Fourteen years later it is very clear. God, my Heavenly Father, has called me to be an ACTIVIST!

And guess what? I'm not alone. He's called you to be one, too.

Don't let the word *activist* scare you! We all have different views of what an activist does and is, but as you look at the life of Jesus and read what Scripture says we are to be, there is no better word to describe what your life and mine should be. Throughout the Bible, you and I are called to be activists of love, community and forgiveness, activists for the hurting, the poor and the lost. As we look at the life of Jesus, we will find that He is the fighter for and defender of those things, and you and I are called to be and do the same.

It is time to look at yourself differently, throw away all limitations and see who you really are. It might be the most challenging thing you will ever do, but it is worth it.

I look forward to enjoying the journey with you, my fellow ACTIVIST!

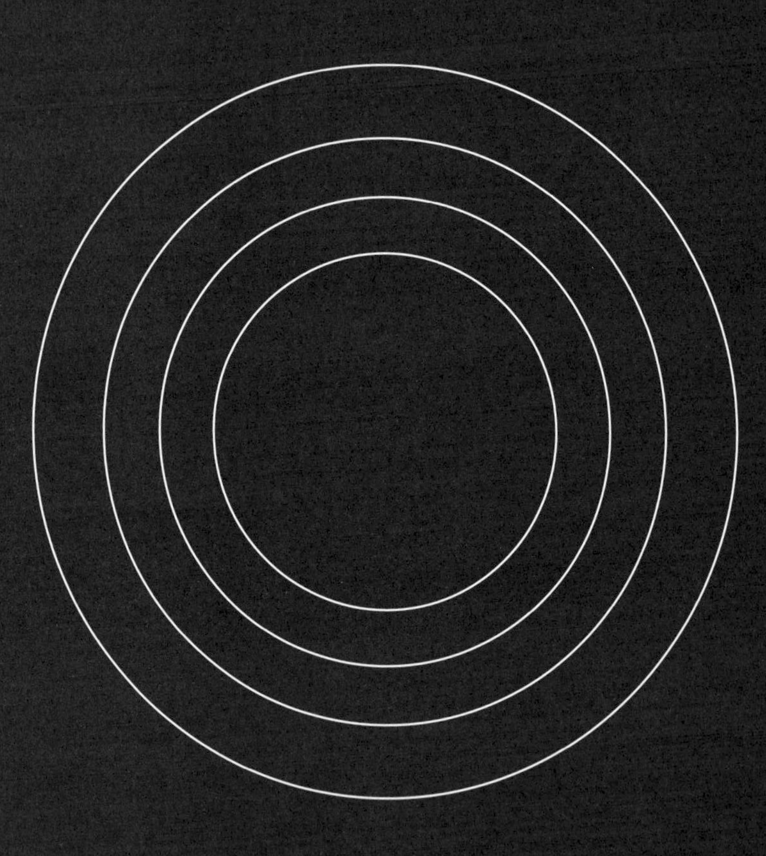

CHAPTER ONE

THE ULTIMATE ACTIVIST

CHAPTER ONE
THE ULTIMATE ACTIVIST

AC•TIV•IST

(noun) - an especially active, vigorous advocate of a cause

There is something inspiring about watching people fight for a cause. The truth is, most of the movies we watch and books we enjoy are about someone seeing an injustice in the world and fighting against it. It doesn't matter if we are talking about fictional stories like *Harry Potter* or true ones like *The Blind Side.* We cannot help but be drawn to someone taking action and changing lives. We pay billions of dollars to read about it and see it. It pulls emotions out of us we didn't even know we had. There isn't a single person reading this that hasn't envisioned themselves being the hero and saving the day. It is a dream within all of us.

Who isn't moved when they hear the story of Mother Teresa? She spent 45 years in Calcutta, India, caring for the poor, sick, orphaned and dying. She was an activist for the helpless, and because of her example, many others have been challenged and inspired to do the same with their lives. But you don't have to live in India to see people in need of help and those counting on God's people to take action. Mother Teresa inspired the world to help where they could, and her example impacted people around the globe.

We love hearing, seeing and reading about activism. We have all watched others change the world. Yet, therein lies the problem.

While all of us love to watch others fight for a cause, sadly, many of us sit back and do very little ourselves. We may give a little money, cheer, cry and be emotionally moved by a cause, but most of us won't truly engage or fight for one.

Why is that?

If there is something deep within that draws us to change the world—and we have the opportunity to do it—why do many of us never do it? Why don't we throw our lives into something big—or even something small—

that will make a lasting impact? Why don't we strive to be part of making a difference that changes how people see the world and perhaps God? While there are probably a hundred reasons why most of us go with the flow and live with an *it-is-what-it-is* attitude, when it all boils down, the truth is that most of us don't want to pay the price.

Being someone who fights for the things Jesus does, whether in their community or halfway around the world comes at a cost. And let's be honest, for most of us, that cost is a bit high. We aren't willing to put ourselves out there and see what happens. We aren't willing to sacrifice so much that it hurts. We like living comfortable, good lives.

Now, in the spirit of being honest with each other, if the attitude I just mentioned is where you find yourself today, and you want to stay there, then stop reading. Put down the book and walk away! Consider it my gift to you. I want to save you the time it takes to read this.

However, if you are still with me—and I bet most of you are—then the reason for that is simple: You have a driving desire to change things, and you have something worth committing your life to fight for. You see injustices in the world or even at your school that you were created to fix. Deep within you is a driving force—a purpose, a reason for your life and your very existence. Most people today do not know what that is or even where to find it.

To start, many of us need to look at our lives differently. You are not just here on earth to take up space, float your way through life or make the most money you can. Your life is worth much more than you could imagine, and if you are willing to count the cost and pay the price, the world awaits in eager expectation to experience what the ACTIVIST inside you will do!

ACTIVIST

Activist. The word alone puts pictures, images and thoughts into our heads. You and I may see different things, but when we hear the word, it brings images of action and pictures of movements that have shaped the world. Society is what it is today—in fact, the entire world is what it is—because of people who chose to move out of the norm and change things around them. These activists were people who believed in something GREAT! Many times they believed in something that was far greater than anything anyone in their time had ever believed in, something that moved people to a cause much greater than themselves. They were moved by great conviction, motivated by an enormous drive of what is right, true and even godly in nature. They stood out, spoke out and lived a life that they believed to be right, true and godly. They refused to sit around and watch the injustices of the world.

They were not just part of history, some past moment of significance. No, they are all around us right now. While others have their inner activist lying silently inside themselves, waiting to be awakened, the true activist is planning, living and—most importantly—*doing*. They are changing the world!

From the beginning of time, activists have shaped culture, moved nations and propelled the world to think, behave and react differently. They are the pioneers of defending love, communities and forgiveness. They're fighting for the hurting, the poor and lost. They have an agenda that is not simply for their own benefit. It burns deep from a pull that comes from their soul and heart. It isn't something they invented or came up with in a crazy dream; it is something put into them by something Greater than themselves.

Some might say it is not a case of chasing a cause, but rather having a cause chase them. They simply couldn't run from it any longer. Something had to be done, and they were the ones created to do it. It was their call, mission and reason for life. These people are all around us, and because of their boldness, life has changed. Don't get me wrong, I am not just talking about BIG changes that everyone sees! I am also talking about the small, everyday things Jesus calls us to be an activist for, those things that make just as much difference in people's lives.

I am sure that after reading that description of an activist you probably have someone who comes to mind, probably a celebrity, someone we read about in all the magazines and on the Internet, or a person on the news. But as I said earlier, activists aren't just well-known personalities. They can be everyday people like you and me. Often that is the case.

To clarify the qualities of an activist, I will give you a few easily recognizable examples. Their contributions to the world have been huge, and their causes can be clearly seen.

MARTIN LUTHER KING, JR.

(January 15, 1929 – April 4, 1968)

Who can forget the man that moved civil right forward by having a dream? On August 28, 1963, Mr. King delivered a 17-minute speech that shook the United States. With passion and conviction he spoke to over 200,000 people who believed in the cause he was fighting for. As you read some of his speech you are not just reading some words in a book you are reading what an activist in action looks like.

> *I have a dream that one day this nation will rise up and live out the true meaning of its creed: "We hold these truths to be self-evident, that all men are created equal." I have a dream that one day on the red hills of Georgia, the sons of former slaves and the sons of former slave owners will be able to sit down together at the table of brotherhood. I have a dream that one day even the*

state of Mississippi, a state sweltering with the heat of injustice, sweltering with the heat of oppression, will be transformed into an oasis of freedom and justice. I have a dream that my four little children will one day live in a nation where they will not be judged by the color of their skin but by the content of their character.

I have a *dream* today!

PAUL DAVID "BONO" HEWSON

(Born: May 10, 1960)

Surprised? Bono is the lead singer of U2, a band that has not only shattered several records in the music industry, but also regularly sells out venues all over the world. While that is what he used to be most known for, I would argue today that he is now more recognized for something bigger than just his music. If you go online, you will find much more about what he has done for humanitarian efforts around the world. He is someone who has used his gifting (music) for something much greater than just a rhythm.

Bono once said, "Eight million people die every year for the price of going out with your friends to the movies and buying an ice cream. Literally for about $30 a head per year, you could save 8 million lives. Isn't that extraordinary? Preventable disease—not calamity, not famine, nothing like that. Preventable disease—just for the lack of medicines. That is cheap, that is a bargain."

Bono gets it. He understands it is about more than using his musical talent to sell records and be famous. He understands that the music is a vehicle he can (and does) use to change the lives of thousands. He doesn't only give money, he raises awareness of the conditions millions of people across the globe live in everyday. He has used his influence, money, talents and position to move people to something life-changing.

BILL GATES

(Born: October 28, 1955)

We all know who he is! Bill Gates is making things possible that we couldn't even dream of 10 years ago. Every day you more than likely use some sort of product or device that he has had a hand in developing. Bill Gates is the innovator of Microsoft. Yep, MICROSOFT. You would think that with that checked off on his list he would just kick back and watch the checks roll in, but that is not at all the case. After his work with Microsoft had earned him several billion dollars, can you guess what he spends his money on now? Bill Gates along with his wife are activists.

As of 2007, Bill and Melinda Gates were the second most generous philanthropists in America, having given tens of millions of dollars to charity. They give millions to education in the United States as well as bring medical supplies to countries that need it. Bill Gates is yet another activist who saw beyond using his money to only take care of himself. Instead, he is using it to take care of millions of people he has never met. Talk about changing lives!

MILLARD DEAN FULLER

(January 3, 1935 – February 3, 2009)

You may have not heard of him, but his contributions to this world are immeasurable. He was a businessman, lawyer and self-made millionaire by the age of 29. May not sound like too big of a deal, but what he did after all the success and money was huge. In 1968, he gave up his wealth to focus on something greater than the money. In 1973, he and his family moved to the Congo and became missionaries. Then just a few short years later he started a little non-profit we all know as Habitat for Humanity. By 2003, Habitat affiliates worldwide had built over 150,000 homes and were active in 92 nations. Millard Dean Fuller had activist written all over him. He saw what could be and should be and made it happen.

Here is one more example of an activist. You probably not have heard of him but I can tell you personally that what he is doing in India is changing countless lives this very moment.

DWAYNE WEEHUNT

(Because I know him, I won't reveal his age!)

In January 2009, I found myself on a plane headed to Mumbai, India, to see a friend's ministry in action. Dwayne started Sower of Seeds International in 2001. He and his team are nothing short of amazing. They build water wells, support schools, care for orphans and much more. What he and his team are doing through their work has saved countless lives. Dwayne is an activist for people around the world who don't have a voice of their own. It is an honor to serve with him. Later in this book, I will give you a chance to be a part of this vibrant ministry that is reaching so many.

Finally, I have to mention the ultimate activist that ever lived. While the people I listed above have had tremendous impact, the truth is that there is One who has done much more than any of them could ever dream. His life, His activism, will be the foundation for this book. What He was an activist for, I believe we should be activists for as well.

JESUS OF NAZARETH

I don't think this came as a huge surprise to you, but if it did then welcome to the story of Jesus. He is and will always be the greatest activist the world has ever seen or known. As you look throughout Scripture you will find Him healing, feeding, teaching, caring, mentoring and even saving people's lives. He is the ultimate activist of love...not only thousands of years ago but even to this day. He is the biggest activist you have fighting for you even if you don't accept it or know it. He is someone who counted the cost and was will willing to pay the greatest price. Many people have become numb to Jesus' story. They have forgotten how big His story is!

The other day, I asked a student, "What did Jesus do for us?"

He responded, "He died for our sins."

Good answer, but he said it as if he was ordering a pizza. He may as well have said, "Hey, thanks, Jesus for the Cross and stuff. No big deal, I will make that whole death thing up to you later."

Jesus did something for you and I that is far deeper emotionally and spiritually for us than I could ever describe. The sacrifice He made on our behalf—the chance to be right with God—is immeasurable. To know that I would have an activist fighting and dying for me so that I may have life is amazing. It is amazing because I know me. I know my mistakes, things I think about, my selfishness. I know me, and I will bet if you are honest with yourself, you know you, too. As humans, it isn't pretty to look at what we have become. Yet through all the sin, shame and guilt, Jesus saw each of us and became our ultimate activist on a cross. He did something for you and I that we will never be able to repay. He gave His life so you and I could have life now and eternally. He saw everything you have ever done and still chose to come to your rescue even before you asked Him to. He sees all and knows all and loves us unconditionally. You cannot make Him love you more or less than He already does. He has given you His full measure of love and nothing can change that.

While you and I will never be able to repay what our activist did for us, there is something Scripture says we should do, something that is our only reasonable response to His sacrifice. Paul writes in Romans 12:1-2, *"Therefore, I urge you, brothers and sisters, in view of God's mercy, to offer your bodies as a living sacrifice, holy and pleasing to God—this is your true and proper worship. Do not conform to the pattern of this world, but be transformed by the renewing of your mind. Then you will be able to test and approve what God's will is—his good, pleasing and perfect will."*

Paul is saying because of all God has done for us, we should be living sacrifices. A living sacrifice is someone who lives their lives open and ready to follow God's call and leading. God's call and His leading are about showing people who He is and loving them no matter where they live or what stage of life they're in. It is Him working IN our lives, THROUGH our lives and WITH our lives to bring glory and honor to the only One deserving of it. Paul's teaching is a plea for us to stop looking at this world and acting like it. Instead, we're to look above this world and react to what we hear. When we do that, something truly amazing happens, we become living activists for the causes of God.

Being a living activist is what this whole book is about! It isn't about making the front page of the paper or being on TV. It is about living your life in a way that people cannot help but be changed forever. Being a modern activist isn't about being the next Bono or Bill Gates. It is about you and I seeing what Jesus was an activist for and how that plays into our everyday lives. If we are open, willing and ready to pay the price, if we simply care about the things Jesus did, we will radically change everything and everyone around us. It isn't about doing one huge thing. It is about everyday ordinary little things that Jesus did when no one was around or cheering. Most activists aren't seen or read about. They spend their days not even thinking about being an activist; it is just who they are. Their voices and actions are loud, not because they are in a picket line or rally, but because they are empowered and released by God for His purposes.

Throughout the rest of the book we are going to look at the life of Jesus and follow His trail of activism. Scripture says we should be emulators of Christ and that is what being a living activist is all about—living as Jesus did! But it's not without challenge. There will be a cost, and the price is high. The things that mattered to Jesus were the difficult things—love, forgiveness, our communities, the poor and the lost. That gets messy, but that is where God's love is needed the most.

My hope is that as you see Jesus' example, it will inspire and motivate you to take up those same causes. Because when you do what Jesus did and love the same things He does, the world changes. It is time to stand up and stop watching the world go by. You are called to be an ACTIVIST. It is time to start living like it!

CHAPTER TWO

ACTIVIST FOR LOVE

CHAPTER TWO
ACTIVIST FOR LOVE

"Jesus loves you!"

Few people who read this book have never before heard those three words. Personally, I have grown up hearing them. I have heard them from pastors, parents, strangers in restaurants and even from a homeless man on the corner who shouted it through my car window. I have seen those three words spoken with laughter and cheering, and I have witnessed them choked out through tears and surrounded by silence.

Having heard it for most of my life, of course, I believed it. And I still do.

Jesus loves **YOU!**

But even as I write that, I realize that it puts me in a weird spot, a place many people live. We know that Jesus loves *you.* We're just not so sure that He really loves *me.* Basically, I believe the statement when it goes to others, but not when it comes to me. Sounds strange, right? Where does this doubt come from?

For me, it comes from knowing every bad thing that I have thought about. It comes from knowing the real intentions of many of my "good deeds." I know the things I've taken that weren't mine to take. I know that when my life is compared to what God desires it to be, I fall short. In fact, I don't even get close!

You may be reading this and believe I'm over-thinking this whole deal, but let's look at what Scripture has to say.

In Exodus 20 Moses brings down the 10 commandments from Mount Sinai. This was huge. God had spoken to Moses and he was returning from the mountain to deliver God's Word to the Israelites. Those commandments were more than just a set of rules. They were directions straight from God himself about how the Israelites should live, all written out on two stone tablets. Take a look:

THE 10 COMMANDMENTS

1) **Exodus 20:2-3 – I am the Lord your God, who brought you up out of the land of Egypt, out**

of the house of slavery; Do not have any other gods before me.

2) Exodus 20:4 – You shall not make for yourself an idol, whether in the form of anything that is in heaven above, or that is on the earth beneath, or that is in the water under the earth.
3) Exodus 20:7 – You shall not make wrongful use of the name of the Lord your God, for the Lord will not acquit anyone who misuses His name.
4) Exodus 20:8 – Remember the Sabbath day and keep it holy.
5) Exodus 20:12 – Honor your father and your mother, so that your days may be long in the land that the Lord your God is giving you.
6) Exodus 20:13 – You shall not kill/murder.
7) Exodus 20:14 – You shall not commit adultery.
8) Exodus 20:15 – You shall not steal.
9) Exodus 20:16 – You shall not bear false witness against your neighbor.
10) Exodus 20:17 – You shall not covet your neighbor's house; you shall not covet your

> **neighbor's wife, or male or female slave, or ox, or donkey, or anything that belongs to your neighbor.**

Did you read them closely? Did you notice anything about all of them? Here is what I noticed about what God was saying and how each of those commandments looks in my life:

1) **God demands to be first in every area of my life. Yes, I've blown that one!**
2) **I'm not supposed to make idols. Well I have never made an idol out of wood or melted down gold, but I have made idols out of other things.**
3) **I have spoken the "G.D." word too many times to count!**
4) **Sabbath what?...**
5) **Not only have I disrespected God, but I have lied to, cussed at and said I hated my parents.**
6) **While I haven't killed anyone physically, I have killed plenty with my words.**
7) **Adultery? Well technically I have never done**

that, but Jesus explains later in Scripture that *"technically"* isn't all there is to that one.

8) **I have stolen more stuff than I can recall… Don't even get me started on how many Internet songs I've illegally downloaded.**
9) **I have lied about friends and others to get what I wanted.**
10) **To top it all off, yes, I look at what others have all the time and cannot help but wish it was mine.**

There it is. I have admitted the ugly truth about myself. Honestly, I feel a little better, but that doesn't really change a whole lot.

As you can see, I am nowhere close to lining up with where God's commandments and His standards are set. So now maybe it makes a little more sense as to why I can say Jesus loves YOU, but I have a hard time with the "me" part!

Of course, many might say, "Andy, that is Old Testament stuff. I am pretty sure a bunch of that changed when Jesus came onto the scene." You are right...in a way. Along with Jesus came the New Covenant (or agreement).

Let's take a journey and see how Jesus compares the old with the new. One thing I learned rather quickly is that Jesus tends to raise the stakes.

Look at Matthew 5:27-30, *"You have heard that it was said, 'You shall not commit adultery.' But I tell you that anyone who looks at a woman lustfully has already committed adultery with her in his heart. If your right eye causes you to stumble, gouge it out and throw it away. It is better for you to lose one part of your body than for your whole body to be thrown into hell. And if your right hand causes you to stumble, cut it off and throw it away. It is better for you to lose one part of your body than for your whole body to go into hell."*

In Exodus, God said don't do it, and in Matthew, Jesus takes it to a whole new level. He said you might need to cut something off. He is telling us that it is better to enter heaven with missing pieces than end up being a crispy critter.

It's kind of funny to me that I have had countless people ask me if Jesus really meant to actually cut something off or gouge something out! The answer is no. He is making a point and using these examples to help you see how important this is. Think of it this way: if that's really what Jesus wanted us to do, there wouldn't be a teenage boy alive with eyes or hands! (Sorry, I had to throw that one in there.)

Back to the point, Jesus is saying that when we look lustfully at someone else, we have already committed sin! Honestly, I cannot recall how many times this very thing has happened with me. I've never improved my odds of hitting the mark God set for me. So once again, the same question returns: *Jesus loves you, but how can He love me?*

I wrestled with the answer to this for years until I realized something. Jesus can love me in all of my mess-ups, failures and selfishness because He is, at His core, an activist for love. It is what moves and lives within Him. It is who He is and what He does in the midst of our brokenness and in the midst of our victory.

But even knowing that, it has still taken me a long time to begin to take hold of the love Jesus has for me. Perhaps it felt too good to be true. I have a wife and daughter whom I love more than I ever thought possible, but the type of love we are talking about—the type of love Jesus has for each of us—is infinitely bigger than anything I could have on my own.

Could God really love me enough to see all my sin and shame and still want to do something about it? Could He still want to make me right with Him? *Yes.* How can we be sure? It comes down to one moment in time: Jesus on the cross.

You have probably heard the story of Jesus and His death on the cross many times. In fact, we just looked into it a little in the previous chapter of this very book. But let's go a step further. We believe what Jesus did for everyone else, but it's time to start believing that He did it for you, too. He has demonstrated His love for ALL of us in the most irreplaceable way. Jesus loves you and me. It is who He is and what matters most to Him. But it doesn't stop there. The love He has for others is also the greatest thing He has called you and I to be an activist for.

In Matthew 22, Jesus was asked a great question and within the answer lies the heart of Jesus and what matters most to Him. Matthew 22:34-39 says, "*Hearing that Jesus had silenced the Sadducees, the Pharisees got together. One of them, an expert in the law, tested him with this question: 'Teacher, which is the greatest commandment in the Law?'*

"Jesus replied: 'Love the Lord your God with all your heart

and with all your soul and with all your mind.' This is the first and greatest commandment. And the second is like it: 'Love your neighbor as yourself.'"

This isn't just something Jesus said because it sounded good; it was what His entire life revolved around. I have heard it said that everything God has done for His people is rooted in love. Jesus proves that to be true. Look at everything He taught and did while He was on this earth. His love affects each of us. His love working through our lives has the ability to change everyone and everything around us. And changing people's lives is what an activist is all about.

I opened this book with the subject of love because love is the most important thing to be an activist for, and it is also the hardest. But if we allow love to operate in our lives, every other aspect of being an activist will fall into place. If the love of God and others is what we are all about, huge change *will* happen.

Still, it's a difficult process. Loving a God who has been good to you and given you life is one thing; loving a stranger or somebody who drives you crazy is another. God tests me in this area on a regular basis. If you're like me, you often find yourself around a lot of unlovable people. They can be mean, they lie, they gossip and they just outright make life hard. Sometimes I think I am starting to get a little better understanding of what hell must be like. Surely, I'm not alone. You don't have to look very far to come across difficult people. They are everywhere—hurting, angry and looking to make other people feel as miserable as they do. But they didn't start out that way. In most cases, difficulties started to shape them. The old saying, "Hurting people hurt people," is just as true today as it was 100 years ago. The good news is, there is an answer for how we can still be an activist for love even to the seemingly unlovable people around us.

CAN LOVE CONQUER ALL OR WAS SOMEONE LYING?

Jesus was surrounded by people who were hard to love, some of whom were the closest to Him. He handpicked His disciples. He invested in them, taught them and gave those 12 men a front row seat to the greatest events in the history of mankind. Even so, Jesus' disciples were hard to love sometimes. Just look at the famous dinner, or Last Supper, He had with them. This had to be the most eventful dinner ever, and certainly the one artists have had the most fun painting. Jesus gathered all of His 12 disciples and started a conversation that quickly turned south.

> *When evening came, Jesus was reclining at the table with the Twelve. And while they were eating, he said, "Truly I tell you, one of you will betray me." They were very sad and began to say to him one after the other, "Surely you don't mean me, Lord?" Jesus replied, "The one who has dipped his hand into the bowl with me will betray me. The Son of Man will go just as it is written about him. But woe to that man who betrays the Son of Man! It would be better for him if he had not been born." Then Judas, the one who would betray him, said, "Surely you don't mean me, Rabbi?" Jesus answered, "You have said so." – Matthew 26:20-25*

Jesus was having dinner with a close, trusted friend all the while knowing that the friend had sold Him out. Not only did he sell Him out, but he set Him up to be arrested and eventually killed! That's how you know Jesus was the real deal. If I were in that same position, let's just say that love would be the furthest thing from my mind. I have watched enough prison shows to know, "You snitch you get a stitch." Jesus, cool as ever, continued to break bread with them and even had a sing-a-long with His guys (verse 30).

As if that wasn't enough, in chapter 26, another disciple let Jesus down in a major way, too. Earlier, Jesus had told His disciple Peter that when things went down, Peter was going to deny ever having known Him. Of course, Peter's response was nothing short of shock and disbelief. But sure enough when the time came, it happened just as Jesus said. Even in this event, love shined past all darkness. Jesus knew what had to happen so that He could show His ultimate love for you and me.

I have always been puzzled by Jesus's ability to love others who talked about, lied to, betrayed, denied and eventually killed Him. I know that love is important, but isn't there a justifiable end to love? Apparently not. First Corinthians teaches us what love is—what it looks like, what it does and what it doesn't do.

First Corinthians 13:4-8 says, "*Love is patient, love is kind. It does not envy, it does not boast, it is not proud. It does not dishonor others, it is not self-seeking, it is not easily angered, it keeps no record of wrongs. Love does not delight in evil but rejoices with the truth. It always protects, always trusts, always hopes, always perseveres. Love never fails.*"

When I read that passage, it screams out what Jesus was all about and what we should be about as well. Love never fails; it can conquer any heart, situation, need or person. The more you love those hardest to love, the more you understand God's heart and what Jesus lived out on this earth. Loving others at all times could be the hardest thing you will ever do in your life, but the reward is earth-shattering.

LOVE IS THE CATALYST FOR ALL ACTIVISTS

Love is the foundation for all living activists. It is the motivator and reason for what we do as activists, and without it, we will fail. Everything will be for nothing. Let's take a look at what Paul teaches us in 1 Corinthians 13:1-3:

> *If I speak with human eloquence and angelic ecstasy but don't love, I'm nothing but the creaking of a rusty gate. If I speak God's Word with power, revealing all his mysteries and making everything plain as day, and if I have faith that says to a mountain, "Jump," and it jumps, but I don't love, I'm nothing. If I give everything I own to the poor and even go to the stake to be burned as a martyr, but I don't love, I've gotten nowhere. So, no matter what I say, what I believe, and what I do, I'm bankrupt without love.*

You and I are bankrupt without love. If we do all these great things here on earth and don't do them out of an overflow of God's love to us, they are worthless. Love is the catalyst for all activists. Love changes everything and everyone.

I started off this chapter assuming you would have been told at some point in your life that Jesus loves you. But honestly, part of me hopes that this revelation may be new to you and that you have been changed by it. It is the absolute truth: Jesus loves you. Throughout this chapter,

I have given you the Gospel or good news of Christ! I've told you about the love and forgiveness He has for you. He really does love YOU! That isn't preacher-speak or some feel good pep talk. It is truth that is proven and backed up.

Without a doubt, there are people reading this who have never experienced the love of God through His Son Jesus. If you are going to be an activist that changes everything, it starts with coming into a relationship with the ultimate activist. You must first know love and be shown love to truly give it out to a hurting, broken world. Perhaps this is your time to experience something you never had before—true, unconditional love—love that changes everything about your life now and forever.

If you want something you have never had, you have to do something you have never done. If that is where you find yourself now, I invite you to connect your heart to God and give Him everything. Then watch as you gain more than you could ever have imagined. It all starts with you inviting Him to invade your life. Ask Him now. The activist that was planted inside you the very second your life began is dying to get out!

CHAPTER THREE

ACTIVIST FOR COMMUNITY

CHAPTER THREE
ACTIVIST FOR COMMUNITY

I will never forget years ago when I received my first invitation to speak at a big conference. There weren't four or five people attending, but well over a hundred. The topic was on trends and technology. I was really excited and made sure everything was prepared from the videos I was going to show to what I had planned to talk about for my part of the session. Things started out great, but towards the end of my speech, they headed south.

It was time for the Q&A, and I took questions from other pastors and youth workers in the room. I never really like Q&A sessions because I prefer situations that I can control and predict. So there I was, answering questions, when from the back of the room an older gentleman stood up and asked about the role the Internet would play in churches in the future. Remember, this was years before Facebook. We were still on Xanga. This being a topic I was very excited about, I unleashed every possible idea that was floating in my head. I said youth groups would meet online. I said there would be small groups that people could join through their computers or phones. I said people from around the world would be small group leaders to these students.

As I was saying all of this, I was thinking, "Man, I am really on a roll here!" In my own little world I was knocking it out of the park. I decided to end with this, "Community has changed and location plays a small role anymore."

This sounded awesome to me, and to this day, I still stand behind it 100%. But in my session, this was the point when I sensed that my audience was less than thrilled with what I had said. Then it began—mumbling. Out of nowhere, one guy stood up and said, "That ain't community!"

From the other side of the room, another said "That isn't a real friendship!"

Right in front of me, a woman asked, "What about the creepers?!"

Needless-to-say, this was not what I expected. The audience in my head was full of cheering fans. The truth is, I didn't win too many over that day. In fact, I was never invited to speak at that conference again. (Note to self: Next time avoid the Q&A session.) While I learned a good lesson about reading my audience that day, I can now see that there was a totally different lesson with regards to becoming an activist.

COM•MU•NI•TY

(noun) - people with common background

When people think about community, most have it wrong. Like my audience that day, they want put things into small compartments where everything looks nice and neat, but when it comes to community, that simply doesn't work.

Look at the definition of *community* closely: "People with a common background." A common background could be anything from race to hometown to the video games you play. Community happens when people connect, and people generally connect through common experiences. With today's technology, it is very possible to have community with people you have never met face-to-face. Millions are doing it. People are getting hired for jobs through video chat interviews, buying houses on the other side of the world from realtors they have only talked to online and, some people are even getting engaged before their first meet-up. The first time they see each other face-to-face is on their wedding day. (That last one is a little weird, if you ask me, but it happens all the time!)

In the definition of community, the important word is *common*. Yes, sometimes opposites do attract, but most likely, you and your community have things in common like movies, music and clothing styles or something bigger like spiritual beliefs, political views or major life experiences. When you and I connect with people via online or on a baseball team, they become our community. And trust me, community happens everywhere.

Of course, it's important to point out that while community is happening everywhere, *healthy* community isn't. We all have some sort of community; it's part of our very DNA as humans to need it. Unfortunately, many have it with the wrong group. They have little to no effect on the community in which they live. Or possibly, they have an effect that is not beneficial. Of course, this is nothing new. Just open the Bible; you won't have to turn too many pages to find unhealthy community. It's negative and destructive wherever it exists, and it isn't long before people within it, as well as those nearby, begin to experience harsh realities. It's like putting poison in the water. It's harmful to everyone.

So how do we fix this? We are called to be activists for *healthy* community. Surely, you could see that point coming, but don't take it lightly. Being an activist for healthy community is very hard to do. Many fail because they don't pay attention to the most important aspect: people. God has called us to fight for and put it all on the line for the right people in our lives. This is vital. If you look in Scripture, this was Jesus' approach, and while times have changed, His principles for being an activist for community have not.

Through Jesus' life, you can see His focus not only on the large community around Him but also the small one close to Him. Let's look at how He made a massive, positive impact on both.

FINDING HEALTHY MENTORS

As you follow the relationship Jesus had with His disciples, you will see He always taught and invested in them. He did something that has been lost—He mentored them. Jesus came along side them and showed them the way.

How about you? Do you have someone speaking into your life right now? Someone teaching you and helping you see things clearly? Someone guiding you into the things of God? Do you have people you trust and depend on to help get you through good and bad times?

Having a healthy mentor has been an unbelievable asset in my life. I've had several mentors for years. I have mentors for money, God, ministry and even family. These men speak into my life and help me develop into the person God has called me to be. Without them, I would not be where I am today, and you wouldn't be reading this book. Having a mentor, or mentors, in your life changes everything! Trust me, there aren't many things more powerful than people praying, guiding and teaching you about places they have already been in life and things that they have already experienced.

Finding a mentor isn't as hard as you think. In fact, every man I have ever asked to mentor me has said yes. People are usually flattered to know someone looks up to them. You will find many are willing to teach you.

But having a mentor doesn't just benefit you, it also benefits the mentor. Men and women all around us are looking for opportunities to use their gifts to help others. Don't get discouraged if you do ask someone who isn't interested. The worst that can happen is that they say no, and you find someone else. Trust me, there are plenty of others out there! Find people you respect, that have good character and have accomplished things similar to what you want to accomplish.

Recently, I had a student come to me and tell me that he wanted to do the same thing I do. Honestly, I was shocked because I didn't know if he even knew what it was that I do. I eventually discovered that he wanted to learn how to speak on stage. I was flattered! Believe it or not, I don't get that request from students very often, so when I do, I take full advantage of it. He had seen what I did and wanted to do the same. Hopefully he will do it even better than me one day.

Look around you. Do you see a coach, teacher, pastor, youth leader, businessman, athlete, writer, speaker or actor that has done or is doing the things you are passionate about? Do you see people you would like to be like? People who could speak into your life? Do they have good character and godly judgment?

Recently, I met a mentor on a trip to Guatemala. He is 10 years older than me, works at a church twice the size of mine and does the same job I do. From the moment I met him, I wanted to learn from him, and trust me, I'm definitely learning. He is able to walk me down the path, helping me avoid the pitfalls, and I am eternally grateful for him.

As I said earlier, I like to have mentors speak into various areas of my life. I have another mentor that makes millions of dollars. No, he and I are *not* alike in that area, but he has been speaking into my life for over 10 years, helping guide me in what to do with my money.

So what about you? Who is pouring into your life? Who around you could teach you things that would take you years to figure out on your own? Jesus was the ultimate mentor to His disciples, teaching them in the good times and in the times full of mess-ups.

Look at the mentoring that happened with Peter. Jesus had just finished feeding five thousand people and sent the disciples off ahead of him. Meanwhile, He stayed and finished up with the crowd. It was then that one of the most famous Bible stories occurred. Matthew 14:25-31 says:

> *Shortly before dawn Jesus went out to them, walking on the lake. When the disciples saw him walking on the lake, they were terrified. "It's a ghost," they said, and cried out in fear. But Jesus immediately said to them: "Take courage! It is I. Don't be afraid." "Lord, if it's you," Peter replied, "tell me to come to you on the water." "Come," he said. Then Peter got down out of the boat, walked on the water and came toward Jesus. But when he saw the wind, he was afraid and, beginning to sink, cried out, "Lord, save me!" Immediately Jesus reached out his hand and caught him. "You of little faith," he said, "why did you doubt?"*

I have heard this story a thousand ways, but it rarely looks good on Peter's side. I happen to think of this story differently than most. To my way of thinking, Peter, at least, stepped out of the boat! No one else there even attempted to walk on the water. So I don't see this story as a failure on Peter's part. Instead, I see Jesus, in a few short sentences, showing us what a mentor does. Mentors call you to something great. If you fail or don't totally get it right, like Peter, then your mentor is there to pick you up, teach you what you may have missed and move on beside you. Being an activist for community means being willing to fight for having the right mentors in your life. Start today! Find a few mentors and see how fighting for the right things in your life can change everything.

THE CLOSE COMMUNITY

Jesus' community consisted of twelve men He handpicked to be His disciples. We can learn from this because most of us join groups where we fit in, but Jesus personally chose His few from the crowd. Look at how His selection went down in Matthew 4:18-22:

As Jesus was walking beside the Sea of Galilee, he saw

two brothers, Simon called Peter and his brother Andrew. They were casting a net into the lake, for they were fishermen. "Come, follow me," Jesus said, "and I will send you out to fish for people." At once they left their nets and followed him. Going on from there, he saw two other brothers, James son of Zebedee and his brother John. They were in a boat with their father Zebedee, preparing their nets. Jesus called them, and immediately they left the boat and their father and followed him.

We don't know the details of why or how Jesus chose each of His disciples, but obviously He wasn't just looking for people to hang out with. He was looking for people who would change the world. Jesus was very selective of those in His close community.

Just as with Jesus, our close communities are the friends and people we choose to surround ourselves with. We are all smart enough to know that our friends shape who we are. The problem, however, is that many people don't think their friends are poor influences on them. If they did, then they wouldn't hang out with them! Now remember, community happens with people you share a common background. This means you have some sort of bond with another. Bonds are not easily broken, but sometimes they need to be.

Scripture has several things to say about the people we hang out with. Proverbs 13:20 says, *"Walk with the wise and become wise, for a companion of fools suffers harm."* Far too many of us have been walking around with fools for far too long. It's time to closely look at the community we spend most of our time with and ask: Are these people bringing me closer to God or pulling me further away? The answer to that question will tell you what you should do. By the way, don't think that just because you go to church with someone that they are a good influence. Some of the worst influences in my life came from a church youth group! Can I get an AMEN?!

This close community called your friends is extremely important, so make sure they are the right people. It is great to know as many people as you can, but remember, close friends shape you.

COMMUNITY-AT-LARGE

While there are small communities in which we live most of our lives, there is another community we are called to be activists for. It is the city or town in which you live. While Jesus had His twelve close disciples, He also spent a lot of time within the community helping, healing, feeding and teaching.

Look at what Jesus did shortly before Peter walked on water with Him. John the Baptist had just been beheaded, and Jesus was heartbroken. Notice the interaction between Jesus' close community and the community at large in Matthew 14:13-21:

> *When Jesus heard what had happened, he withdrew by boat privately to a solitary place. Hearing of this, the crowds followed him on foot from the towns. When Jesus landed and saw a large crowd, he had compassion on them and healed their sick. As evening approached, the disciples came to him and said, "This is a remote place, and it's already getting late. Send the crowds away, so they can go to the villages and buy themselves some*

> *food." Jesus replied, "They do not need to go away. You give them something to eat." "We have here only five loaves of bread and two fish," they answered. "Bring them here to me," he said. And he directed the people to sit down on the grass. Taking the five loaves and the two fish and looking up to heaven, he gave thanks and broke the loaves. Then he gave them to the disciples, and the disciples gave them to the people. They all ate and were satisfied, and the disciples picked up twelve basketfuls of broken pieces that were left over. The number of those who ate was about five thousand men, besides women and children.*

In the midst of His pain, Jesus couldn't help but have compassion on the community-at-large. If Jesus felt love like that for people He had never met in the middle of such personal pain, don't you think His example is important to follow? Surely, it was not easy for Him, and He had to fight through it. Just as Jesus fought through His pain to help people in need, we should do the same. We live in a society where the general thought is "mind your own business," but come on! God has placed us in a city or town for a reason. We have gifts and abilities to contribute, to make our community better, to change others within it, to feed those without or to help those who are helpless.

It is time to get involved with your community and do what only you can do to make a difference. Stop being lazy and saying you don't know what to do or where to start. Call an organization, church or non-profit outreach. Places are always looking for volunteers. Or, get creative and innovative, and start something yourself. Just walk outside and look around; need is everywhere. Make the most of opportunities. You can do more than change the color of a house; you can change the person who lives in it.

Several years ago, I was working with an organization that took hundreds of teenagers to a small town and totally changed the community by serving it. They painted houses, fixed roofs and did countless other tasks. They did it with great joy and loved it even more than the homeowners they were helping. They gave all they had, and in return God filled them up more. I will never forget that summer when students, just like you, decided to change a community. By the end of the week, not only had houses been changed, but the lives of the people had been transformed. Relationships were built.

Opportunities like this come up every day. Be a part. Jesus was. Let me ask you again: How does your community see you? Sadly, most communities don't see us at all. Why not? Why don't they see students working to bring change? Why don't they see activists?

ENGAGE YOUR COMMUNITY

Your community isn't limited to a specific location anymore! Through the Internet, you can find close friends and mentors. I am sure some of you already have friends in other countries that you have never met in person. Your community can be larger now than at any other time in history. You *can* help people and communities around the world, and I will tell you how later. Don't forget how important it is to have the friends that live 5 minutes away from you as well. The ones you can see face to face and laugh or cry with. They are very important and many times are the ones that are there for our weakest moments and our greatest victories. For now, just understand that your community matters. Who is around you and speaking into your life, whether they are 1,000 miles away or two feet away, shape everything about you. It is time to act. That is what activists do and what this book is all about!

Now go out there and find a few mentors. Who knows, you might even have to use Google translator to speak with them. Fight, seek out and ask God for mentors and friendships that draw you closer to Him, friendships that challenge you to be all God has called you to be. An activist for healthy community has the ability to go further than they ever dreamed possible.

CHAPTER FOUR

ACTIVIST FOR THE POOR

CHAPTER FOUR
ACTIVIST FOR THE POOR

I grew up in a pretty affluent suburb outside of Oklahoma City. There weren't any homeless people on the street corners. I am not even sure our town had a shelter for people when it got cold. Most of my friends lived there, too. When I was sixteen, my parents did what I thought every good parent should do. They gave me a car. Life was good for me and it was just as good for the people I hung out with. I didn't see much poverty. If there were people in need around me, I didn't notice. My parents always made sure I had money for gas, food, clothes or whatever else I may have wanted. The older I get and the more bills I pay, I see how fortunate I was. I know I am not painting a very good picture of myself, but I want to be transparent about where I came from and where God has brought me.

Now that I'm older, I realize that there are people with needs all around. All you have to do is open your eyes and look. The older I get the more need I see. A few days ago I was stopped at a light, about to get on the highway, and I saw a man with a sign that read, "Hungry, Please Help… God bless you." I sat there wondering if anyone was going to help! No one did and about 20 cars, including mine, passed him by. While driving down the road, I started to wonder how that man got there. How do things get so bad you cannot afford to eat and your only option is to stand on the side of the road and beg? What must it feel like to have everyone stare at you and judge you thousands of times a day? Honestly, a million things could have happened to bring him to that place. Surely, he didn't plan on spending his life being hungry and depending on the change of others.

Now that I am well past my teenage years, seeing people in need like that turns something within me. Maybe it's because, for a long time, being a compassionate person was not at the top of my list.

God has been developing compassion in me for years. Like many, I can be very selfish. Yet through grace and mercy, God has shown me the joy of giving—not giving just money, but time, too. Becoming an activist for the poor means selflessly giving of your time and resources to show others the greatness of God! It's not so you can be on the front page of the paper. It's about having a heart for the things that mattered to Jesus. Look at what He taught in Matthew 6:1-4:

> *"Be especially careful when you are trying to be good so that you don't make a performance out of it. It might be good theater, but the God who made you won't be applauding. "When you do something for someone else, don't call attention to yourself. You've seen them in action, I'm sure—'playactors' I call them— treating prayer meeting and street corner alike as a stage, acting compassionate as long as someone is watching, playing to the crowds. They get applause, true, but that's all they get. When you help someone out, don't think about how it looks. Just do it—quietly and unobtrusively. That is the way your God, who conceived you in love, working behind the scenes, helps you out" (The Message).*

Isn't that last sentence great? God is working behind the scenes to help us out, and He is also using us behind the scenes to help out others. All we have to do is open our eyes and look around to see opportunities to be an activist for the poor. Throughout Scripture, we find that Jesus had unbelievable compassion for the poor and needy. He was their defender and provider. This is what we should do, too, both locally and around the world.

About a year ago, I had a life-changing experience. While I have traveled a lot, I had never been to India. Our group had been raising money for Sower of Seeds Ministry for a few years, and now it was time to go see some of the work being done. I didn't know what to expect. I had seen the movie *Slum Dog Millionaire*, but that was about all the preparation I had going for me. Workers there warned me that I would never see the world the same after visiting, but I didn't take their warning seriously.

After almost 9,000 miles, my plane landed at 2:45 a.m. I thought most people would be asleep, but much to my surprise, I saw a mass of people at the airport. On our way to the hotel, I saw even more people—more than I could have ever imagined. People were everywhere, and it was still pitch dark at 3 a.m.! This didn't even come close to the crowds that were there during the day. It was just the tip of the iceberg.

The next morning, the team picked me up, and we headed out to see several sights. I was shocked by what I saw. Never before had I seen so much need. Kids were running around naked in the street. Kids with their hands cut off were begging for money. We later had the opportunity to hang out with some street kids who had found a way to survive. They had formed their own community and way of survival by relying solely on each other. It was crazy. Really crazy.

There were so many poor and needy people there that words cannot describe. I was speechless, which is rare for me. One day, they took me to see and play with orphans who either have AIDS or are HIV Positive. As I looked into the faces of these children who had done nothing to deserve their pain and suffering, I saw something even more shocking—joy. These children with such hard lives were filled with joy. They smiled and laughed. They tugged at my pant leg begging me to come see their rooms, which they were so proud of. There was so much joy in the midst of their pain. That joy came in part from activists who gave so much.

When I finally made it back to my hotel, I was emotionally drained, confused and determined to do more. That is one reason I am writing this book. I want to bring awareness and give you the opportunity to be part of changing the world, both where you live and in places you will never set foot. The poor and needy were at the top of Jesus' list, and they should at the top of ours, too.

Look at the parable found in Matthew 25:31-46. Try and put yourself in the story. Ask yourself: *Where would I fall?*

> *When the Son of Man comes in his glory, and all the angels with him, he will sit on his glorious throne. All the nations will be gathered before him, and he will separate the people one from another as a shepherd separates the sheep from the goats. He will put the sheep on his right and the goats on his left.*
>
> *Then the King will say to those on his right, 'Come, you who are blessed by my Father; take your inheritance, the kingdom prepared for you since the creation of the world. For I was hungry and you gave me something to eat, I*

was thirsty and you gave me something to drink, I was a stranger and you invited me in, I needed clothes and you clothed me, I was sick and you looked after me, I was in prison and you came to visit me.'

"Then the righteous will answer him, 'Lord, when did we see you hungry and feed you, or thirsty and give you something to drink? When did we see you a stranger and invite you in, or needing clothes and clothe you? When did we see you sick or in prison and go to visit you?' "The King will reply, 'Truly I tell you, whatever you did for one of the least of these brothers and sisters of mine, you did for me.' "Then he will say to those on his left, 'Depart from me, you who are cursed, into the eternal fire prepared for the devil and his angels.

For I was hungry and you gave me nothing to eat, I was thirsty and you gave me nothing to drink, I was a stranger and you did not invite me in, I needed clothes and you did not clothe me, I was sick and in prison and you did not look after me.' "They also will answer, 'Lord, when did we see you hungry or thirsty or a stranger or needing clothes or sick or in prison, and did not help you?' "He will reply, 'Truly I tell you, whatever you did not do for one of the least of these, you did not do for me.' "Then they will go away to eternal punishment, but the righteous to eternal life.

Are you catching what Jesus tried to communicate? Who are the "least of these?" The poor and needy. Whether locally or globally, we are called to be activist for these people. It is about you and me seeing a need and doing something about it. In the final chapter of this book, I am going to tell you where you can start helping and share stories of people who are truly activists for the poor. These people and organizations get what Jesus was talking about.

How about you? Is something starting to click within you? Are you looking at the poor and needy differently? If not, perhaps your prayer can be for God to develop more compassion in your life. After all, you never know how close you are to being the one on the side of the road holding the sign.

COMPASSION IS AT THE CORE

"Compassion is sometimes the fatal capacity for feeling what it is like to live inside somebody else's skin. It is the knowledge that there can never really be any peace and joy for me until there is peace and joy finally for you too."

– Frederick Buechner

As I mentioned earlier, God is constantly working on the area of compassion in my life. It isn't that I don't care about the poor or needy; I just don't think about them and their needs as much as I should. Everywhere Jesus went, He had compassion on the people He came in contact with, except maybe the Pharisees and Teachers of the Law. Even when times were tough and He may not have felt like it, Jesus was consumed with compassion. Remember the story in Matthew 14? Jesus had just heard that John the Baptist had been beheaded by Herod. Can you imagine what Jesus felt at that moment? Yet follow a few verses down in Matthew 14:13-16 and look at how He handled the pain and loss!

When Jesus heard what had happened, he withdrew by

boat privately to a solitary place. Hearing of this, the crowds followed him on foot from the towns. When Jesus landed and saw a large crowd, he had compassion on them and healed their sick. As evening approached, the disciples came to him and said, "This is a remote place, and it's already getting late. Send the crowds away, so they can go to the villages and buy themselves some food." Jesus replied, "They do not need to go away. You give them something to eat."

In the midst of pain and loss, Jesus saw people with needs, and He put those needs above His own. That's something we all need: to look at others and their needs and to put them above our own.

In Matthew 22:37, Jesus gave the two greatest commandments: "*'Love the Lord your God with all your heart and with all your soul and with all your mind.' This is the first and greatest commandment. And the second is like it: 'Love your neighbor as yourself.'*" Loving your neighbor who lives next door can be hard enough, but loving the unknown neighbor who lives half-way around the world is another. That, however, is our calling from God. We should see a need, get filled with compassion and do something about it.

One interesting point about the story is that even the disciples tried to get Jesus to send the people away. He responded by telling them to give the people something to eat. The disciples wanted the people to find food themselves, but Jesus said that they would meet the people's need. One chapter later in Matthew 15:32, He was at it again: *"Jesus called his disciples to him and said, 'I have compassion for these people; they have already been with me three days and have nothing to eat. I do not want to send them away hungry, or they may collapse on the way.'"*

Jesus loved feeding people. He fed 4,000 the second time. Eating is the most basic need people have. Everyone must eat, or they will die. Meeting basic needs has always been one of the greatest ways to reach people. Missionaries do it all the time. They aren't asking for new cars and houses, they are asking for water wells and used shoes. Others are asking for a dollar a day to feed children who would otherwise not have a meal.

Missionaries are some of the most compassionate

people I have ever or will ever meet. They have given up their lives to serve and meet the needs of people. That isn't everyone's calling, but being compassionate and doing our part to help the poor is!

Even as I write this book, I am working on another talk for a fundraiser in Southlake, Texas. It is for an organization called Community Storehouse. It meets the needs of people by providing food and clothing. It currently helps thousands of people with the compassion of Jesus and makes a huge difference. Without organizations like this, many more people would be holding signs, asking for food.

Surely, the town or city you live in has an organization like this. Find it and start helping today. You can do it right now! Once you get out there and start meeting the real needs of the poor and needy, you will be filled with a joy like never before. Something powerful will stir within you when you put aside selfishness and give out of compassion and love.

CHAPTER FIVE

ACTIVIST FOR FREEDOM

CHAPTER FIVE
ACTIVIST FOR FREEDOM

Whenever I hear the word freedom, America always comes to mind. It is a country where you are free to become just about anything you want and a place where opportunity is everywhere. While there is a lot of freedom in America, many of us aren't *really* free.

How can we live in the United States and not be free?

It's simple. While we have the freedom to go anywhere we want and do the job we like, many of us are trapped and enslaved by things we have done, things we believe or things that have happened to us.

Let's look at some of the things that may be holding you back from becoming the activist you were born to be. Some of these things may have been in your life so long you may not even realize they are there. Others affect you every day. It is time to change all of that! It is time to go deeper into what the Ultimate Activist gave you when He died on the cross—FREEDOM!

FREEDOM FROM ADDICTIONS

You may know John 3:16 by heart, but when was the last time you read the verses after it? In them, Jesus gives us a spiritual truth and challenge.

For God so loved the world that he gave his one and only Son, that whoever believes in him shall not perish but have eternal life. For God did not send his Son into the world to condemn the world, but to save the world through him. Whoever believes in him is not condemned, but whoever does not believe stands condemned already because they have not believed in the name of God's one and only Son. This is the verdict: Light has come into the world, but people loved darkness instead of light because their deeds were evil. Everyone who does evil hates the light, and will not come into the light for fear that their deeds will be exposed. But whoever lives by the truth comes into the light, so that it may be seen plainly that what they have done has been done in the sight of God. —John 3:16–21

Jesus starts off giving us the good news about what God has done for us. Then He explains why God did it, and then He shares the idea of living in light or darkness. He challenges us to come into the light and stop hiding in the darkness. He wants us to stop lying, to live by truth and righteousness and to refuse to hide any wrongdoing! Sounds easy, right? Wrong!

Many of us have addictions that are taking away our freedom. We all know about the big, bad addictions—medications, drugs, pornography, alcohol. Those are the ones people talk about, but what about the lesser known addictions—acceptance, an unhealthy relationship, food, media, gossip? On what have you become way too dependent? What can't you imagine living without? What is in your life that shouldn't be there?

Maybe you can't think of anything, and that is ok. There is still a principle you can learn and take with you in the future. Others know exactly what I'm talking about. Whatever the addiction might be, Jesus has the answer. While quitting is hard, it is an important step toward true freedom.

There are three things you can do right now to gain

your freedom. They are practical and understandable but very hard to do. Trust me, if you put this into practice, things *will* change.

First, bring the addiction to God. Be honest and tell Him what is going on and ask for forgiveness. You may not think you deserve it or even believe God will give it, but the truth is found in 1 John 1:9: *"If we confess our sins, he is faithful and just and will forgive us our sins and purify us from all unrighteousness."* None of us deserve God's forgiveness, but that forgiveness is part of the love of the Ultimate Activist. It is time to stop running from God and start turning to Him.

Second, bring the addiction out of the darkness and into the light by telling others about it. It is time to stop hiding and face this head on. You might tell your parents, friend, pastor, youth leader or even trusted teacher. When you bring things from the dark side of your life into the light, something awesome starts to happen—the addiction loses power. Some addictions have been hiding so long they are eating you up inside. It is time to do something that is uncomfortable and freeing all at the same time. Talk to someone you can trust but also someone who can help.

Third, get accountability. Find a person you can talk with about your struggles, someone who can call you out. They are the ones who are watching what you are doing and encouraging or correcting you along the way.

I have talked to hundreds of students over the years who don't mind telling God, but hesitate to tell others. They don't want someone calling them out, so they walk away. Unfortunately, they usually walk right back into whatever they were doing.

Remember, we bring our struggles to God, to others and then we get accountability. That may seem short, sweet and difficult, but it's a great place to start. Honestly, for some your process may be God, others, accountability and REHAB! I am not sure, but God is sure! He will help you.

FREEDOM FROM LIES

Do you believe lies about yourself or others? Have you believed negative words people have said about you, like you are a nobody or a loser? Do you struggle with the fear of failure or not being good enough? Do you fear of being too young to accomplish what God wants to do in you? Before the activist inside you can be unleashed, you must be free. Galatians 5:13-14 says, *"You, my brothers and sisters, were called to be free. But do not use your freedom to indulge the flesh ; rather, serve one another humbly in love. For the entire law is fulfilled in keeping this one command: 'Love your neighbor as yourself.'"* In our freedom, we are called to serve and love one another. Scripture cries out for us to be the activist for others.

FREEDOM FROM UNFORGIVENESS

The last trap I want to talk about that holds back many people is unforgiveness. It can keep you from being the person God called you to be. This is a difficult step, but forgiveness is so important.

A few years ago, I had been hanging out with a fourteen-year-old student, Mike (not his real name), for a little over a year. We got to know each other pretty well, I thought, until one day he opened up and shared some deeply personal and painful information about his biological father. I knew he didn't live with his dad, but that's not uncommon. More than half of the students I know have dads who have checked out.

As he began to talk about his father, it was obvious that Mike was really hurting. He told me that he had never met his dad, or at least not that he could remember. Mike's dad was an absent father, to say the least, and had some drug issues to go along with that. As I looked into Mike's eyes, I saw years of pain and anger (and rightfully so). A few weeks later, I received a phone call from Mike's mother. Mike's dad wanted to meet him and start a relationship. That afternoon I sat and talked with Mike about what it might be like to meet his real dad for the first time. It was intense. I had Mike write down some questions he had for his dad. Mike wanted to know, "Why did you leave us?" "Why did you not come back for me?" "Why were drugs more important?" He had other questions too, but they are too personal for me to mention here.

After he left my office, I sat and stared at his questions. *God, what do I do now?* I wondered. I was lost on what to say, but I couldn't help but believe that this could be the moment for healing to begin for a scared, questioning boy who grew up without a dad.

A few days later, Mike agreed to meet with his biological father for the first time. I cannot explain the nervousness that filled the room. Mike and I talked for about 30 minutes before his dad arrived. I could still see the anger, but it was now mixed with some excitement and fear of what might happen. Who knew how this was going to go down? Would they fight? Scream "I hate you!"? I wasn't sure. I just knew that Mike would regret it if he didn't meet him.

"You ready" I asked.

"Not really," he answered.

"Well, it's time."

With that, I went outside with only one request for Mike's father. Mike didn't want any physical touch from his dad. No hugs. No handshakes. *No problem,* I thought.

I left the room and went to talk with Mike's dad for a few minutes. Then I opened the door to where Mike was sitting. Words can't describe the emotions and tension that filled that room. They both stood and stared at each other for a few seconds with tears in their eyes. Before I could do anything, they embraced each other and years of bottled up emotions rolled down their faces. I had officially blown it in the no hugging department, but I assumed it was ok.

Seeing a boy meet his dad for the first time was a deeply spiritual experience for me, but the hard part was yet to come. How should they move forward? Mike's questions rolled out of his mouth, and his dad did his best to answer them. His sorrow and regret were obvious. Almost an hour of conversation went by, and I thought it could not have gone any better. With that, they stood up and hugged again, and Mike's dad walked out the door. As the door shut, Mike looked at me and asked, "Why did you let him hug me?"

I didn't know how to explain to someone so hurt that forgiveness was the answer. Mike had no reason to forgive his father. The damage his father had inflicted on him was already done. It would be difficult to fix. Mike had every right to be mad, angry and sad all at the same time. Yet the one thing I knew was that forgiveness may not be deserved, but it had to come for healing to occur.

That happened years ago and Mike is still working it out the best a teenager can. I am very proud of him. Asking him to forgive his dad was asking the world of a fourteen-year-old. As for his dad, he left the scene as fast as he had entered it. Mike hasn't heard from him since. My heart breaks for Mike, but I know he will overcome this. He cannot hang on, hold on, be bitter, hate or live in anger and still expect to move forward.

So what about you? Are you in the middle of a situation that seems too big to be forgiven? Has a friend lied to you or gossiped about you? Did your dad leave? Has someone abused you? I could go on, but you can fill in your own injustice. We've all experienced injustices like these, but leaving them unresolved holds us back from being the activists God has called us to be.

So what does activism have to do with forgiveness? Let's review the definition of an activist: *an especially active, vigorous advocate of a cause.* There is no greater cause than forgiveness. It is what Jesus came to give you, and throughout Scripture, you can see how it completely changed people. Your life, in fact, is radically different because of it.

When most people think of an activist, they think of a person fighting for something. They think of some injustice that needs action. Forgiveness is worth fighting for, and quite possibly, it is the action that will combat the injustice you have endured.

Right now, you may have so much unforgiveness in your life that it is incredible. You may have been hurt, scared, embarrassed, let down, talked about. Did I miss anything? Forgiveness may be the last thing you want to think about, but that is the very reason why you should be fighting for it more than ever.

WHY MOST AREN'T ACTIVISTS FOR FORGIVENESS

There is something deep within us that always wants to be right. A lot of times we will lie, cheat or even steal just to be so. We love having the upper hand, because it gives us a sense of power.

Growing up, I had two older brothers who loved to

punish and torture me in any way possible. They were much bigger and would team up on me. I still have issues and phobias today because of them. Most of their torture was good, old fashioned, brotherly love, but sometimes they would go too far and really hurt me, which would cause me to totally shut down. I wouldn't talk to them, and they would know that they had gone too far. They would apologize, but I would still keep an attitude of unforgiveness. They'd continued to try to make things right, and I'd continue to stay angry. What was I really doing? I was withholding forgiveness in order to control the situation. This happens all the time. Act angry and hurt, and out of guilt people treat you better than before. Yes, it is a sick and twisted world, but as I said, we all want the upper hand.

Your situation may be different. Your unforgiveness may have nothing to do with power or the need to be justified. You could be so angry and in so much pain that forgiveness isn't even on the radar. I don't even want to imagine the situations you've faced. I have worked with students for 14 years now, and I have heard horrific stories. Those students didn't deserve or ask for what happened to them. Like them, you may feel helpless, hopeless and angry. You may want to know why that terrible thing happened or why that person hurt you. I won't try to understand all that has happened to you, but know that moving forward is hard to do when your heart is filled with unresolved hurt.

Sometimes the hardest person to forgive for really dumb mistakes is yourself. It is much easier to forgive others than to forgive the one you can't escape from. A few years ago, a student asked me what the biggest mistake I ever made was. There have been millions. Picking just one was hard. I sat back and thought for a few minutes. I came to the conclusion that it wasn't one or two mistakes; it was six years of them. I, like so many others, made the mistake of wasting my middle and high school days. God gave me influence, and I didn't use it in a good way. That's something I can never get back.

What about you? What keeps you from being an activist for forgiveness? Whatever it is, it is time to forgive and let go. Don't let it hold you back any longer.

JESUS' THOUGHTS ON FORGIVENESS

Jesus was the ultimate advocate for forgiveness, and we can learn a lot from what He said about it. In Matthew 18:21-35, He answered some tough questions about this very topic.

Then Peter came to Jesus and asked, "Lord, how many times shall I forgive my brother or sister who sins against me? Up to seven times?" Jesus answered, "I tell you, not seven times, but seventy-seven times.

"Therefore, the kingdom of heaven is like a king who wanted to settle accounts with his servants. As he began the settlement, a man who owed him ten thousand bags of gold_ was brought to him. Since he was not able to pay, the master ordered that he and his wife and his children and all that he had be sold to repay the debt. "At this the servant fell on his knees before him. 'Be patient with me,' he begged, 'and I will pay back everything.' The servant's master took pity on him, canceled the debt and let him go. "But when that servant went out, he found one of his fellow servants who owed him a hundred silver coins. He grabbed him and began to choke him. 'Pay back what you

owe me!' he demanded. "His fellow servant fell to his knees and begged him, 'Be patient with me, and I will pay it back.'

"But he refused. Instead, he went off and had the man thrown into prison until he could pay the debt. When the other servants saw what had happened, they were outraged and went and told their master everything that had happened. "Then the master called the servant in. 'You wicked servant,' he said, 'I canceled all that debt of yours because you begged me to. Shouldn't you have had mercy on your fellow servant just as I had on you?' In anger his master handed him over to the jailers to be tortured, until he should pay back all he owed. "This is how my heavenly Father will treat each of you unless you forgive your brother or sister from your heart."

The first question you might ask is: "Seventy times seven equals 490, right? So I should start keeping tabs on my friends right now, because it won't be too long before they reach that."

That, unfortunately, is not the meaning. Later Jesus began to tell the story of one person who had been forgiven of debt. He had received grace and mercy. You would expect him to extend that same grace and mercy to others but he didn't. In fact, he did the exact opposite. Not a good choice!

Jesus was trying to teach us to forgive others for their sins and mistakes, just as we have been forgiven by God. We shouldn't focus on a number of times to forgive, but rather we should extend forgiveness whenever and wherever it is needed.

Jesus said it another way in Matthew 6:14-15: *"For if you forgive other people when they sin against you, your heavenly Father will also forgive you. But if you do not forgive others their sins, your Father will not forgive your sins."*

Of course, forgiving is not forgetting. You may have the scars—some physical, some emotional—that keep you from forgetting what happened. You cannot forget someone molesting you or physically beating you, but you can heal and move forward with forgiveness, grace and mercy.

Jesus understands what forgiveness of that magnitude takes. He faced the most horrific death that anyone could imagine. It was much worse than any movie could portray it. There He was completely blameless, without sin, never having wronged anyone and yet He hung on a cross, paying the price for the sins of the world. While He hung there, He called out to God the Father, saying, *"Father, forgive them; for they don't know what they do" (Luke 12:34).* He gave the ultimate forgiveness for you and me! Shouldn't we fight for the same thing? What other response could we possibly have than to do as Jesus did and forgive others no matter the hurt?

WHAT DOES AN ACTIVIST FOR FORGIVENESS LOOK LIKE?

Examine your own heart and ask God to uncover any forgiveness issues you have. He will show you, if you ask. Once you find one, start working through it. It may not happen overnight. Just like Mike's forgiveness, it's a process. Find a counselor, pastor, mentor or someone you trust and talk through it. Trust me, it will help.

If you need to forgive yourself, I encourage you to find out what Scripture says about you, not what your bitter mind can conjure up. At times, you may feel like you're wasting your time, but know that God will shape things within you to help others. Believe the truth in God's Word, not the lies that your mind keeps repeating!

And if you need to ask someone to forgive you, then it's time to admit your error. Perhaps you said something about them or did something to them. Countless relationships could be healed if we would simply pick up the phone and say three simple words: "I am sorry." You might need to apologize to your parents, coach, teacher, pastor, friends or someone else. No matter who it is, start today. You will be surprised how much you will be respected and forgiven.

Forgiveness is a powerful God-idea that we should be activists for! Jesus was an activist for forgiveness, because forgiveness changes everything.

Start right now. Fight for something significant. It's the very thing Jesus died for.

CHAPTER SIX

ACTIVIST FOR THE LOST

CHAPTER SIX
ACTIVIST FOR THE LOST

Marty and I have been best friends for over 15 years. Right after we graduated high school, we became roommates. Shortly after that, God took me on one path and Marty on another. I moved away for my first "real job" at a YMCA camp, and Marty started a construction company. Maybe that is why we remain close friends, I am not good with a wrench, and he can make a living with it. I was his best man at his wedding, and he was mine. I have never met a more generous, giving person in my life. We have both stuck by each other in hard times, like the time I was with him when he found out he had cancer. I will never forget sitting next to his bed in a hotel room in Kansas City talking about life and what it all meant. Marty is a fighter; he never gives in. I respect him for that. For a living, we do totally different things, yet for some reason, we have always clicked. I believe it is a God-thing, but Marty would argue differently. Since this is my book, I will defend my stance, and there is nothing he can say about it! He will just have to read this section knowing that he can't control what I'm going to write!

Long before Marty and I even knew each other, God set things in motion. While we share a lot of common interests like going to the lake, cars and watches, one thing we never see eye-to-eye on is God. My best friend is an atheist! That's right: a pastor's best friend, the person he confides in and trusts more than just about anybody, doesn't believe in God or the existence of any deity. Or as I like to say, he doesn't believe in God YET! Yes, I have tried all the Bible tricks and EvangiCubes. None have worked, and even through the toughest times of his life, he neither blames God nor gets angry at Him. Marty always picks himself up no matter the situation.

It's important to point out that Marty supports and respects what I do. Two years ago, I invited him to watch me speak to a rather large group of teenagers. He walked into the auditorium packed with more than 5,000 people and—right in front of a youth group—he said, "Holy s***! This place is huge!" Like I said, he isn't much on the spiritual side of things, but I couldn't help but laugh at the expression on his face while being surrounded by so many followers of Jesus. I bet he thought we gathered up every Christian kid and put them in one place.

My dream that night was for Marty to meet a true and living God and give it all up for Someone greater than himself. It didn't happen, but I cannot help but get excited for when that day comes. I believe that when Marty and God meet, you will have one of the most generous followers of Jesus this world has ever seen. I believe God will do more through him than He has done through me. I believe one day that my best friend will be set free, redeemed and have a huge kingdom impact. It will happen, even if it is when we are both at the nursing home. An atheist may be what he is today, but one day all that will change. Until then, my best friend doesn't know Christ… YET. I will be an activist for his eternal salvation and for all of those who are in the same place as him.

Jesus was passionate about the lost. While on earth, He loved steering people to the right place. Look at the parable found in Luke 15:1-7:

Now the tax collectors and sinners were all gathering around to hear Jesus. But the Pharisees and the teachers of the law muttered, "This man welcomes sinners and eats with them." Then Jesus told them this parable: "Suppose one of you has a hundred sheep and loses one of them. Doesn't he leave the ninety-nine in the open country and go after the lost sheep until he finds it? And when he finds it, he joyfully puts it on his shoulders and goes home. Then he calls his friends and neighbors together and says, 'Rejoice with me; I have found my lost sheep.' I tell you that in the same way there will be more rejoicing in heaven over one sinner who repents than over ninety-nine righteous persons who do not need to repent.

Even now, Jesus loves the lost, those who don't know Him yet. As an activist, we should love them, too. For me, this is an easy thing to get excited about! I love presenting Christ in a variety of ways and watching people "get it." This happens on stage but also in daily life. The reason I get so fired up about the lost is because I know personally how much better their lives would be with God.

I know Marty doesn't see any benefit to having the Holy Spirit working in His life, but one day he will. He will see what it is like to be comforted by a true and living God. He will experience peace like never before, and there are things that have trapped him that will no longer keep him captive. It isn't about adding another number to heaven; it is about the life he can have now and the hope he can have when his life here is done.

ALL AROUND

Those who don't know Christ yet are all around us. They are at our schools, work, movies; you name it. You cannot avoid being around people who are lost. Even if you spend all your time at church, you will still find those who are lost there. If you don't, it might be time to find a new church! This means that you and I have a daily opportunity to put the activist for the lost into action. I am not saying we go around with tracts and free Bibles every day, but sometimes, that is the answer. I am saying how we live and the choices we make show people what we believe. Asking the right questions and engaging their interest is a great place to start.

I've already told you about my best friend, but he isn't the only atheist in my life. My neighbor is an atheist as well. He's awesome—funny and very intelligent. He has been part of creating several well-known video games and cutting edge electronics for kids. Whenever we get together, we always have a good conversation. We talk about world events and what they mean. He is South African, so our conversation is from an international point of view, not only an American one. We both like BBC News (a British news channel), but we rarely agree about President Obama's politics or healthcare. I especially enjoy our conversations about God. I respect him, and he respects me. I know if he reads this, he will say I need to keep praying because his salvation is never going to happen. So, I guess I'll keep praying, because, like Marty, one day it will all make sense and come together.

What about you? Has God placed someone in your life for you to impact directly? Jesus tells us very clearly that lost people are all around. Who are you praying for and going after? In Matthew 9:35-38, Jesus sums this up:

Jesus went through all the towns and villages, teaching in their synagogues, proclaiming the good news of the kingdom and healing every disease and sickness. When he saw the crowds, he had compassion on them, because they were harassed and helpless, like sheep without a shepherd. Then he said to his disciples, "The harvest is plentiful but the workers are few. Ask the Lord of the harvest, therefore, to send out workers into his harvest field."

It is an exciting thing to watch someone's life change forever. There isn't anything like it. It's amazing to watch God do what only He can do, changing people's lives and calling them to give up everything else to follow Him. There's nothing like seeing lives changed, futures altered and people discovering who they really are and how great God really is. Nothing symbolizes this more than the story of the prodigal son in Luke 15:11-32.

There was a man who had two sons. The younger one said to his father, 'Father, give me my share of the estate.' So he divided his property between them. "Not long

after that, the younger son got together all he had, set off for a distant country and there squandered his wealth in wild living. After he had spent everything, there was a severe famine in that whole country, and he began to be in need. So he went and hired himself out to a citizen of that country, who sent him to his fields to feed pigs. He longed to fill his stomach with the pods that the pigs were eating, but no one gave him anything.
"When he came to his senses, he said, 'How many of my father's hired servants have food to spare, and here I am starving to death! I will set out and go back to my father and say to him: Father, I have sinned against heaven and against you. I am no longer worthy to be called your son; make me like one of your hired servants.' So he got up and went to his father.
But while he was still a long way off, his father saw him and was filled with compassion for him; he ran to his son, threw his arms around him and kissed him. "The son said to him, 'Father, I have sinned against heaven and against you. I am no longer worthy to be called your son.' "But the father said to his servants, 'Quick! Bring

the best robe and put it on him. Put a ring on his finger and sandals on his feet. Bring the fattened calf and kill it. Let's have a feast and celebrate. For this son of mine was dead and is alive again; he was lost and is found.' So they began to celebrate. "Meanwhile, the older son was in the field. When he came near the house, he heard music and dancing. So he called one of the servants and asked him what was going on. 'Your brother has come,' he replied, 'and your father has killed the fattened calf because he has him back safe and sound.' "The older brother became angry and refused to go in. So his father went out and pleaded with him. But he answered his father, 'Look! All these years I've been slaving for you and never disobeyed your orders. Yet you never gave me even a young goat so I could celebrate with my friends. But when this son of yours who has squandered your property with prostitutes comes home, you kill the fattened calf for him!' "'My son,' the father said, 'you are always with me, and everything I have is yours. But we had to celebrate and be glad, because this brother of yours was dead and is alive again; he was lost and is found.'

Someone who was lost was now found. The story of Jesus right before us!

THE LOST DON'T HAVE A DISEASE

Over the years, I have seen Christians avoid the lost. We cling to the idea that we shouldn't associate with them because they could corrupt us and lead us away from God. While this may be true, it's not limited to just the lost. This can happen within the church as well. The lost don't have a disease that you should shy away from. In fact, you should run to them. They are broken humans like all of us. While they may deny God and their need for a Savior, the truth is the truth. The lost need Jesus as much as we do. Instead of turning away from them, we should turn toward them and meet their needs both materially and spiritually. Jesus is a great example of this. In Matthew 9:9-13, He called Matthew, a tax collector, to follow Him.

As Jesus went on from there, he saw a man named Matthew sitting at the tax collector's booth. "Follow me," he told him, and Matthew got up and followed

> *him. While Jesus was having dinner at Matthew's house, many tax collectors and sinners came and ate with him and his disciples. When the Pharisees saw this, they asked his disciples, "Why does your teacher eat with tax collectors and sinners?"*
>
> *On hearing this, Jesus said, "It is not the healthy who need a doctor, but the sick. But go and learn what this means: 'I desire mercy, not sacrifice.' For I have not come to call the righteous, but sinners."*

The sinners, or the non-religious, are who He came to call and be an activist for. You and I are called to do the same. Yes, there are people we shouldn't hang out with, but on the other hand, there are those you are called to influence. This is a tricky balance, but God will show you, if you ask. Don't shy away from the lost. Be drawn to their hearts. After all, you never know when He will change them.

LIVING WITH AN ETERNAL PERCEPTION

It motivates me to know that I am fighting for something eternal, something that will last way beyond the 100 or so years that I live on this earth. If you focus on the things to come, it changes the things that are now. By that I mean, you and I are thinking about what is right in front of us. That changes when we think about eternity and those things that will last forever.

Sometimes it's hard to think much further than the next month, but by focusing on heaven and eternal things, that changes. It's motivating to think about what hell will be like for those who could have been saved. The thought of my best friend Marty living eternally in hell is impossible for me to grasp. It has even kept me up at night. Yes, God draws the lost to Him, but we need to do our part. Our time on earth is so short, and the impact we can make on others lives changes everything.

What about you? Who has God called you to impact for Him? There are people in every follower's life that God has placed there for a reason. Take time and look around. You are an activist for the lost—people who don't know Christ YET, but they will. Pray, seek and know this: what you do and how you live makes a difference. Realize that what you do changes lives and eternity, because even if you don't see it for years, it's happening all around us each and every day!

Marty, I hope you read this and see what God has been stirring within you for years. But even if you don't see it, know I won't stop! God has more for you than you can ever dream. You will be used to change the world and people around you for the greater good of the Kingdom. I hope this book sits at your lake house, and from time to time, you read it and know that someone has been praying for and thinking of you for years. You are a world-changer. I've seen that as long as I have known you. Thanks for being the greatest friend one could ask for. I look forward to spending eternity with you and reminiscing about all the great things God did through us! I know this will happen.

Love you, buddy. I cannot tell you how much our friendship has meant. Thanks for standing by, supporting and loving me and my family. You may be an atheist now, but you are the best atheist I have ever known! For now I will continue to say YET, but I know one day that will change.

CHAPTER SEVEN

THE LIVING ACTIVIST

CHAPTER SEVEN
THE LIVING ACTIVIST

A living activist is someone who uses the gifts that God has given them to stand up and fight for a cause. Not just any cause—a cause that Jesus would stand up and fight for. Remember that being an activist isn't all about rallies and larger-than-life things that people see. It is also the small, behind-the-scenes actions that may never get attention but have a huge impact.

To be honest, that's where God uses us the most.

We all want our own glory sometimes, but being an activist isn't about us. It isn't about what we can gain or be noticed for. It is about what we can give and how we can honor Christ. First Corinthians 10:31 says, *"Whatever you do, do it all for the glory of God."* A living activist knows it is God working in and through them to create change in people and this world. Because of that, it is only fitting for the living activist to give credit where credit is due.

In this chapter, I am going to share several stories with you. They are from young men and women—you might even know them. There may be only one difference between them and you, but it is significant. These people chose to *step out* and be *living activists*—activists of change within their communities, activists behind-the-scenes where God does some of His greatest work.

These stories are meant to inspire you and show you that your life can make a difference. How you live can change so much. While I am only highlighting a few stories, don't think for a second that I couldn't fill an entire book with stories of students who are making differences. Remember: activists are all around us. Are you one?

WALK OF FAITH

Several years ago, I had the opportunity to visit a place like no other. It's called Tennyson Center in Denver, Colorado. It's a school, among many things. Some children live at it, while others commute to it daily. The kids in this school are coming from some horrible backgrounds and living conditions. In fact, when you hear their stories of abuse and neglect, they make you want to cry. Some of the kids have battled abuse their entire lives and without Tennyson Center, they would have little hope.

At the Center, they learn how to cope with anger and painful memories, and they learn life skills. The teachers are incredible despite getting cussed at and threatened daily. The kids themselves are unbelievable as well. While life may have not delivered them the best start, with the help of Tennyson Center and living activists, many have made huge strides and are successes today!

I love taking groups of students there because the experience is life-changing. Students are shocked to walk into the school only to have a five-year-old cuss them out! I have taken many groups to the Center over the years, and most have great experiences. And while they feel really bad about the situation, most students aren't compelled to take any action. I cannot blame them; it is very easy to retreat to their nice homes and video games.

However one visit, in particular, was different. That year I took a group of students who weren't satisfied just sitting around and hoping things would get better. No, they jumped at the chance to become living activists.

Every year Tennyson Center has a Walk of Faith, a fundraiser to improve the Center and keep it operating throughout the year. Great idea, but my students and I live in Texas. It would be a far walk indeed for us to participate in the Center's Walk of Faith! Around 10:00 p.m. on the drive home, I received a call from the van behind us. While my van of students wasn't thinking about ways to change the world, theirs was. One student rose to the top of the movement and started writing down ideas. When we stopped to get gas, Whitney jumped out of the van and ran over and started throwing ideas at me. She talked as fast as she could as she looked over a page of notes. It was clear that her group was serious. Something was going to happen.

They decided that, since Colorado was too far away for them to participate in the Center's annual walk, they would have their own Walk of Faith in Texas. It was a great idea, but it was March and the walk was scheduled for May. With a lot of hard work and possibly sleepless nights,

Whitney and the group pulled it off. They sprang into action to meet a need. The walk rose over $5000 and met the needs of a lot of children. They were, in the truest sense, living activists, fighting for the things that matter to Jesus.

Look at how Jesus valued children in Matthew 19:13-15: "*One day children were brought to Jesus in the hope that he would lay hands on them and pray over them. The disciples shooed them off. But Jesus intervened: 'Let the children alone, don't prevent them from coming to me. God's kingdom is made up of people like these.' After laying hands on them, he left.*"

Whitney and the other students saw a need, something that was important to Jesus and determined to take care of it. What about you? Do you see kids that need help? Do you see places like Tennyson Center where you could volunteer or raise funds? Those are the things activists do!

JOSH KELLY

One of my passions is evangelism! I love it when people hear about what Jesus has done for them. I love seeing them discover the life-changing power of His death and resurrection. I cannot describe the feeling I get when I look out from a stage and see people coming to know Christ in a real way. You can see it in their faces—something has changed and they will never be the same again. Because evangelism is a passion of mine, I love encouraging others to evangelize, too.

Years ago, I met an activist who had the same passion for evangelism as me—Josh Kelly. Josh had come to church with several friends. He wasn't raised in church. In fact, he hadn't been to church before coming to mine. You couldn't help but like his personality and humor. Not having grown up in church, he didn't know the lingo like "washed in the blood of the lamb," or "Do you know that you know?" Everything he had learned from church came from his experience as a teenager. Once he got it, he GOT it! Josh realized who he was and who *He* was.

One night during a service, I asked who wanted to know Christ in a real way. I was shocked to see his hand go up in the air. You could tell he meant it. God had literally reached down from heaven and touched his heart. He stood there with his hand in the air, and I knew that his life would forever change. If you have ever experienced this, you know that God becomes so very real. For Josh, this was and will forever be the greatest decision that he ever made. He changed in that moment, and the Kingdom will never be the same because of it.

That night changed everything for Josh, and he couldn't help but share what God had showed him. We had countless conversations about how to share his newfound knowledge with his friends. Being the spiritual one, I told him it starts with praying for his friends. I know that sounds simple, but I believe that is where it all starts.

Honestly asking God to give you insight and the right words to say to someone who is missing a gaping hole in their heart is always the starting point. After all, the lost or those who don't know Christ yet may not even know they need Him. My best friend doesn't see his need for Christ yet, but I promise you there is something missing in His life he hasn't been able to fill. It isn't that the lost don't desire a relationship with Jesus, but rather, they don't know what they are missing. This is an important point that we in the Body of Christ often overlook. We assume that everyone wants to go to church and understands what God wants to do in their lives. The truth is, many don't understand what Jesus died on the cross for. They see the pictures of the cross, but don't really know what it is about. They see churches and religious people and want nothing to do with them. But keep praying. Their salvation *is* coming!

Josh found what he was passionate about a few months later. For him, having a heart for the lost is where he began. He started praying and bringing his friends to church. At first, many didn't want to come. They thought they knew what it would be like and they thought they knew the kind of people they would meet there. Still, they had seen such a change in Josh that they were intrigued with what had happened. They wanted to know why things were different.

An activist for the lost looks different and chooses differently than others do. They know that their lifestyle and the choices they make influence others. Josh had been the life of the party. Many people liked him and wanted to know how his change occurred. They wanted to know why he was different and why he was making different decisions. It was hard for him at first; many thought he had bought into the "Jesus thing." But after months, he proved that he had changed.

It wasn't six months later that Josh burst into my office and said, "You won't believe this!" With excitement, he began to tell me how God had used him to bring his friend to Christ! It was as if he couldn't believe God would use him to do something that great. And that was only the beginning. Many of his friends started coming to church and making decisions for Christ because of his influence.

Josh was an example of someone who was truly an activist for the lost. It wasn't about money, a rally or starving people in Africa. It was about a heart that had been changed and couldn't help but try to change others. What about you? Do you see friends, parents or others who need to know Christ? Do you see people who don't know Christ yet? If so, *do something*… that is what activists do!

LITTLE THINGS MEAN BIG CHANGE

As I have said, being an activist isn't always about the big things that large numbers of people see. Many times

God uses the small things we fight for to bring about unimaginable change. Throughout the Bible, you will find small acts of obedience and faithfulness that caused huge change. My friend Brian is a great example of how small acts can make huge differences.

Brian was sixteen when he heard sirens wake him up from a deep sleep. He didn't know what was going on, but he knew it couldn't be good. Out his window, he saw his neighbor being rushed into an ambulance. That night, his neighbor died, and the man's wife began a downward spiral. Brian had lived next to them for a few years, but didn't really know that much about them. They only lived ten feet away, yet they were strangers.

Summer was coming, and the grass started springing up. Brian noticed that his neighbor wasn't doing a whole lot to keep it down. One day after cutting his own yard he had an idea: *What if I cut her lawn as well?* It doesn't seem like much, but if you are ever in Oklahoma in the summer, then you know it's a *huge* deal.

All summer Brian cut her grass and never said a word or asked for any money. Yes, I know that is unusual for a teenager, but he felt like that is what God wanted him to do. His neighbor never got out, and he rarely saw her. But something was happening inside her that Brian could have never seen. She had lost her husband of several years, the person she relied on to take care of her, and was struggling to find her place in the world without him. She felt alone, like no one cared. What Brian was doing, unknown to him, was showing her that someone did, in fact, care. She was not alone. When she thought she had lost everything, God used this sixteen-year-old to show her that someone was still looking after her needs.

Don't overlook the significance of Brian's actions. He was a *huge* activist for the things God really cares about. He braved the heat and spent hours showing love and compassion when he didn't have to. Look at what Scripture says about widows, then ask yourself if you think God didn't appreciate what Brian was doing: *"Sing to God, sing in praise of his name, extol him who rides on the clouds rejoice before him—his name is the LORD. A father to the fatherless, a defender of widows, is God in his holy dwelling." –Psalm 68:4–5*

God is a defender of widows! What about you? What

are you fighting for? That summer Brian was the biggest activist on the block, even though he didn't know it. He heard from God, was obedient and showed a neighbor something that she didn't think she would see again—LOVE.

FUTURE ACTIVIST FOR INDIA

In a few weeks, I will be taking six students to India for 11 days. My dream, prayer and goal for the trip is that the experience they have with God and the people of India will change their lives forever. I pray that they might see how the other side of the world works and be moved to compassion. This trip is what I call a game changer, a time that changes everything about you and how you see the world. I believe that these students will look back in 10 years and say that the trip changed *everything* for them, that it was the moment they became the living activists God made them to be.

What about you? When did God speak clearly to you and put a passion inside your heart for something important to Him? Something you were made and created to fight for? We all have passion deposited inside of us. Dig deep and know that God has planted a passion for one of His causes inside of you.

Your cause may not seem big, but you never know how God will use little acts of faith to create great movements of change in this world. Be faithful in helping a neighbor or doing a seemly small thing for someone else. Know that God is honored just as much as if you had raised five million dollars.

God looks at things much differently than we do. We look at how much money we raise or how big the cause is that we're fighting for. God looks at the heart and motivation behind our actions. If you raised five million dollars and it was all about you and your glory, then what was it for…*really?* God is looking for and is ready to work in and through those who know how to give the glory to Him.

Go out there and get started. Students just like you all around the world are living activists for God. They have overcome their fears and any doubts that they can affect change.

In the next chapter, I'm going help you find your passion. I'm going to teach you how to use your gifts to join the fight and become the living activist you were created to be. Get ready!

CHAPTER EIGHT

ACTIVIST OF ACTION

CHAPTER EIGHT
ACTIVIST OF ACTION

Activists are all around us. You don't have to look too far to see them, and I guarantee that your life is radically different because of them. They are the people who refuse to sit and watch the world go by. They are moved and compelled to live a life that fights for the right things—the things that matter to Jesus, the same things that should matter to us.

In this book, we have looked at what Jesus was an activist for. We studied Scripture to see what He valued, lived and taught others. While there are many more things Jesus was an activist for, I think you get the picture of what He was about. He was about loving God and other people. He was about meeting people's needs by feeding them, healing them and having a compassionate heart. As followers of Jesus, that is our call, too. This chapter may be the most important one. It isn't too hard to discover what

Jesus was an activist for, but a bigger question is: ***What will YOU fight for?***

This opens the door for other questions like: Where should I put my efforts? How do I know if I am being used to my fullest potential? Most people who volunteer and help out with a cause do so because they were asked to or even begged to. Often they don't stay long, or they only help out once.

Yes, you should be an activist for everything Jesus was about. But certain causes will move and motivate you far greater than others. There are thousands of great charities and causes to get involved with all around the world, but they are not ALL for you. So how can you discover the cause that matches your life? How do you not burn out after one month or feel like you are wasting your time? It starts with knowing a little about yourself and what makes you tick. You are gifted by God to make a huge kingdom impact. It is time to identify those gifts and find a cause to throw your entire life into.

I am going to walk you through a slightly modified version of a system for discovering your vision that Craig

Groeschel came up with years ago. He, is perhaps one of the greatest teachers on vision and how to uncover yours. By asking three key questions, you will find a cause that burns within you.

YOUR VALUES

The first question is this: What are you about? What are your values? Or let's ask it this way: What things in your life mean the most to you? These are the things you stand for and are willing to fight for. Your values could be family, excellence, integrity, character, hard work, faith, generosity, sacrifice, knowing God, creativity, courage, confidence, evangelism—the list goes on and on. Don't let my list interfere with yours. These are just a few examples of hundreds of values. To help you identify your values, ask yourself: What do I love? What am I willing to fight for? What happens around me that makes me burn with godly anger? It could be an injustice or witnessing someone being devalued. It could be something that is happening or even something that isn't happening, but should.

YOUR TALENTS

The second questions is: What are you good at? What are your gifts and talents? Be real with your answers. It is okay to be conceited with this one. When you close your eyes, what is it that you know you do really well? What are the things you do better than anyone else? (Or at least what things do you think you do better than anyone else?) Maybe it is teaching, leading others, discerning situations, playing a certain sport, communicating, writing or playing music, informing others about injustices, raising money or creating events. Whatever it is, be real and honest. Everyone has something they are good at. Trust me; God will use it.

Austin Gutwein is an activist who used his gifts to make a lasting impact. In 2004, he saw a show about orphans who had lost their parents to AIDS. He was driven to do something. He used his gifts to help raise thousands of dollars. In one day, he shot 2,057 free throws at his school to represent the number of children who would become orphans in one day's time because of AIDS. Who knew that God could use the free throw gifting to raise money?

Think about it: What are you really good at?

YOUR EXPERIENCES

The third question is: What have you experienced? What are the most influential life experiences that you have had so far? So often God uses life experience to prepare us for His work. Some of your most painful situations might just lead to the cause you were created to fight for. If you need help coming up with your most influential life experiences, think of a time when you really learned something. At the end of it, you probably said to yourself, that is something I will never forget, or that was a hard lesson, or what just happened to me was so good I can't believe it! It could be the time someone came to your rescue. Perhaps it was the first time you experienced God's presence, or a time when your actions directly affected someone else's life in a positive way. Think about this; really consider the experiences that have shaped you.

BRINGING IT TOGETHER

Think about what you just wrote down. You just described what you care the most about (your values), things you are good at (your talents and gifts), and your major life experiences. This may not look like much, but take a closer look. Within those three areas, you will find what the activist inside you is ready to fight for.

I'll use myself as an illustration. I love sharing Christ with others and seeing lives changed. Evangelism is a core value of mine. I believe that I am gifted in leading and speaking. A past experience that influenced me was going to church only to have it be boring and confusing. Because of that, my life is naturally bent towards being an activist for the lost. I love creating experiences where people understand Christ and who He is in a way they never have. In a weird way, I am doing that through this book. When you are an activist for something, you cannot help but fight for it, even when you don't realize that you are.

Remember, we are talking about impacting your world now. Don't worry about 10 years from now. Your passion and excitement for causes will change. Right now you may think that what God is showing you is small and unimportant, but just wait. God may be showing you a smaller dream that will lead to something bigger. Take the values, gifts and experiences you have and put them to work! You might be wondering where you can do that. Let me give you a few examples of where you can start your activism today. Remember, these are just a few ideas. There are thousands to choose from.

THE ACTIVIST PLAYGROUND

Don't limit yourself to the things listed here. Pray and seek God for yourself. He will guide you.

One major way activists are very impactful is through the raising of money. They aren't trying to swindle your hard-earned cash; they simply know what to do with it. They can accomplish more with it because of their experience.

The student ministry I work with understands this. We can either work hard and raise $10,000 to support those who drill water wells, or hundreds of us could jump on a plane and try to figure out how to drill a water well ourselves. Which do you think is a better idea?

I have a passion for raising funds, but I don't think of it that way. God has given me a gift for communication, and I'm honored to use it to help advance what He wants. I can't build a house to save my life, but I can get people to donate the money to build one.

What about you? Can you organize a race, event, carwash or battle of the bands? If so, you can help others in greater ways that you can imagine. You have the ability to raise money that will keep people from dying. Get creative. Do something no one else has done. Trust me; there are millions of people waiting for an activist to save their lives.

COMPASSION INTERNATIONAL

(www.compassion.com)

Let me introduce you to two ministries that you can join right now. The first one is called Compassion International. I went to Guatemala with these guys, and I can tell you the workers are awesome! They are all about partnering with you to sponsor a child. Did you know that for just $38 a month you could be the activist that changes a kid's life forever? That money provides healthy food, clean water, medical care, educational opportunities and important life-skills training. And on top of all that, your sponsored child will hear about Jesus Christ and be encouraged to develop a lifelong relationship with God. Through this ministry, God can use you and your talents to change lives. How many children can you sponsor? How many lives will be changed because you decided to act?

SOWER OF SEEDS INTERNATIONAL

(www.sowerofseeds.org)

I am really excited to share this ministry with you. I have worked with its ministers and they are very trustworthy. I have seen first-hand the work they do—it's amazing and something you can be part of right now. One of their projects is Champions for India. Through this project, they give education and food to children, rescue victims of human trafficking, drill water wells, operate a life center for orphaned and abandoned children and so much more. I personally like the $7.77 project. Did you know that every gift of $7.77 can provide water for one person for 30 years? Your life and what you give makes a difference. You may never see the difference you make in person, but that doesn't mean that it isn't happening and that God isn't honored in your faithfulness. Who doesn't have an extra $7.77 lying around every month? Being an activist for the poor is a huge calling, and if we all work together, we can make a change in the world! Start now. Go online or even text "Answer" to 85994. When you do that they will take $10 to make a difference. In a few minutes' time, you can join me as an activist.

Of course, even if you don't have money, you can still be in the activist game. It just takes more creativity. Let's look at what you can do.

MOVEMENTS

With social media taking over so much today, you can bring awareness to causes like never before. You can create fan pages, write blogs, post ideas and spread information. I get at least two requests a day to join some cause. While some hold little to no significance for the world, others matter. There is a difference between starting a cause page for Justin Bieber and one for the AIDS epidemic around the world. The activist within you may work best behind a computer screen, and there is nothing wrong with that. Find ways to bring awareness and rally people around an idea that moves them to action. Lead them to a place they have never been before and watch as you all experience something new.

Maybe you can create videos, post them, and get people thinking about life in a whole other way. YouTube is an awesome place to start, as others before you have. Maybe you can photograph the world and inspire others to action by what they see. Yes, I am talking big ideas, but the problem for many of us isn't that we think too big, it is that we think too small. God said there is nothing impossible (Luke 1:37), so why don't we believe it and fight for things much bigger than us? Get out there and try something new using every gift God has given you. You have nothing to lose but the life that comes with giving up yours… which, of course, is where true life is found.

THE EVERYDAY ACTIVIST

Yes, we've tackled some big ideas. Those are the things that get me going, but let's not lose track of the little, everyday things that change the world. The everyday activist is constantly looking for the things that Jesus did and acts on them. Why not start being an activist for the kid at school who has no one? Why not start being an activist for the widow down the street, the single parent, the homeless man on the corner, the lost people that surround you? The opportunity for activism is everywhere. Are you a part of moving the kingdom forward and advancing the cause of Christ, or do you sit back, believing you can't make a difference?

I can't help but think that most of us want our lives to count, but we never do anything to make them count. The truth is that we can make a difference. No, we can't do everything by ourselves, but we can do something. We can be part of ending hunger, ensuring fresh, clean water and providing medical care, regardless of wealth. Dream of a world like that and motivate others to join us in the journey! Let's live the way we were created to live. Let's do our part and use our giftings to change the world.

Even as I finish writing this book, I hear a story on the news about a group of medical doctors who are in Haiti right now. They are doing exactly what we have been talking about this entire book—BEING LIVING ACTIVISTS! The timing couldn't be more perfect. But before I end, let me leave you with one more thought on being an activist.

The apostle Paul had an unbelievable conversion found in Acts chapter 9! Before his conversion Paul, then known as Saul, intensely persecuted followers of Jesus. He even participated in the stoning Stephen. He wasn't always the model follower of Jesus you might have pictured him as!

Yet one day the Ultimate Activist did what only He can do, change a life from that point to carry through eternity. On the road to Damascus the old Saul would die and the new Paul would become a massive part of history. He spent the rest of his life fighting for the things that mattered to Jesus and ultimately it would cost him his life. He knew the cost and was willing to pay it. He lived his activist life out for the glory of God in a way that his passion can be shown in the following passage of scripture.

Galatians 1:22-24 After all that time and activity I was still unknown by face among the Christian churches in Judea. There was only this report: "That man who once persecuted us is now preaching the very message he used to try to destroy." Their response was to recognize and worship God because of me!

That, fellow activist should be the anthem of our lives. For people to see how we live and what we do with our lives and their response is to look at Someone much greater than us. Instead of seeing what you are doing, they are really seeing Jesus living and working through you. When you and I choose to live a life like that, one day when your time on earth is up you will hear the sweetest words your ears have ever heard when a loving God says "Well done my good and faithful servant, well done!"

Until that time comes, go out there and make the difference, after all that is what you and I were created to do. I look forward to catching up with you one day and we can share all that God has done in our lives. Till then be encouraged and unleash the activist that has been living inside you since the day you were born!